decoupage

decoupage

Using paper to decorate your home

Josephine Whitfield

Photography by Adrian Taylor

southwater

This edition is published by Southwater

Southwater is an imprint of
Anness Publishing Limited
Hermes House
88–89 Blackfriars Road
London SE1 8HA
tel. 020 7401 2077
fax 020 7633 9499

Published in the USA by
Anness Publishing Inc.
27 West 20th Street
Suite 504
New York
NY 10011
fax 212 807 6813

Distributed in the UK by
The Manning Partnership
251–253 London Road East
Batheaston
Bath BA1 7RL
tel. 01225 852 727
fax 01225 852 852

Distributed in Australia by
Sandstone Publishing
Unit 1, 360 Norton Street
Leichhardt
New South Wales 2040
tel. 02 9560 7888
fax 02 9560 7488

© 1997, 2001 Anness Publishing Limited

3 5 7 9 10 8 6 4 2

Publisher: Joanna Lorenz
Editor: Clare Nicholson
Photographer: Adrian Taylor
Designer: Caroline Reeves
Illustrator: Madelaine David

Previously published as *Inspirations Decoupage*

CONTENTS

INTRODUCTION

The dictionary definition of decoupage is the cutting out and application of paper cut-outs to surfaces. The process is very simple and intensely relaxing. I can easily see why decoupage became a pastime for genteel young ladies as it is similar in its intricacy to working a delicate embroidery. I recently attended a course and it was so enjoyable working in a group where moments of talk, when we all showed each other our work in progress, were interspersed with long periods of calm as we quietly snipped and stuck down our decoupage images. The wonderful part about decoupage is that you can pick it up and put it down easily, and that even if you and a friend start with the same designs you will both end up creating something with a different feel.

A lot of the designs for decoupage are based on heavy floral designs of the Victorian era. These have their place but you should not feel constrained by them because you can use any type of paper and a whole range of images. In this book we have brought decoupage right up-to-date and have taken decoupage in its broader view. With over 20 projects for every area of your home, we have used different materials from black and white prints and reproductions of famous paintings to colour photocopies of flowers and interesting shapes cut out of coloured papers. There are also many interesting paint techniques involved in the projects. There are clear step-by-step instructions showing how to decorate your walls, furniture and accessories. Start by simply creating a door plaque with motifs from wrapping paper. You will then be ready to tackle the larger projects such as the stool which is transfromed with multi-coloured squares of hand-made paper. To help you there are complete materials and techniques sections.

I hope this book inspires you to take up your scissors. I can promise you that once you have started, the sheer delight of quietly snipping away will take over your life.

Deborah Barker

HAT TRICK

The zebra motif has a clear outline, making it an easy motif for a beginner. Black and white always look stylish and you can keep your hats looking equally smart in this zebra-inspired hatbox. The lid is painted in wavy lines to echo the zebra's unique markings.

YOU WILL NEED
hatbox
emulsion paint: white and black
large and small paintbrushes
chalk
ruler
small, sharp scissors
PVA glue
clear water-based acrylic satin varnish

1 Give the hatbox two coats of white emulsion using a large paintbrush.

2 Paint a band of black emulsion around the lid using a large paintbrush.

3 When the paint is dry, chalk the zebra stripes on the surface of the hatbox.

4 Paint in the zebra stripes with black paint using a small paintbrush.

5 Replace the lid and measure from the base of the box to the lip of the lid and calculate the height of the motif. Allow for a little space above and below each motif.

6 On a photocopier enlarge the zebra motif at the back of the book to your chosen size. Using small, sharp scissors, cut out enough motifs to fit all the way around the box.

7 Position and glue the zebras in place, making sure they are evenly spaced.

8 Cover the lid with two coats of clear satin varnish. Leave to dry between coats.

9 Varnish the sides of the box and leave to dry overnight before replacing the lid.

SHELL COLLECTION

Reproductions of old natural history prints are a wonderful source for decoupage images. Simply photocopy as many pictures of shells as you like and use them to decorate a mirror frame. The size of the frame can vary, although it is easier to buy a mirror and make the frame to fit.

YOU WILL NEED
reproductions of shell prints
small, sharp scissors
plain paper
low-tack reusable adhesive
pencil
cardboard
craft knife
cutting mat
ruler
wallpaper paste
newspaper
white emulsion paint
medium paintbrushes
PVA glue
hanging fastener
clear water-based acrylic satin varnish

1 Make colour photocopies of a selection of reproductions of old shell prints. Carefully cut out the images using small, sharp scissors.

2 Glue the photocopied shells on to a sheet of plain paper using low-tack reusable adhesive and arrange them in a frame shape, slightly overlapping the shells as you work.

3 Draw around the outside and inside edges of the frame with a pencil.

4 Cut out the shape to make a template and place face down on the cardboard. Draw around the edge of the template with a pencil.

5 Remove the paper with the shells and cut out the cardboard frame shape using a craft knife and a cutting mat. Also cut out a rectangle and three strips of cardboard for the frame back using a craft knife and ruler.

6 Stick the cardboard strips on to three sides of the cardboard rectangle. Mix up a small amount of the wallpaper paste following the manufacturer's instructions. Dip torn pieces of newspaper into the paste and cover the cardboard with two layers of pasted paper. Leave to dry.

7 Paint the frame front and back with white emulsion. Glue the frame back to the frame front with PVA glue. Use heavy books to weight it down.

8 Remove the shells from the paper and glue on to the frame in the same arrangement. Glue a hanging fastener to the back. Apply two coats of varnish.

SCREEN TEST

This screen is decorated with colour photocopies of flowers and leaves, and the scope for different colours and shapes is enormous. The combination of delicate gold tissue paper with pretty dried and photocopied flowers is very arresting.

YOU WILL NEED
unpainted screen
parchment-coloured matt emulsion paint
medium paintbrushes
pencil
tape measure
ruler
tissue paper
gold spray paint
wallpaper paste or PVA glue
scissors
fresh leaves and flowers
craft knife
cutting mat
dried flowers and leaves
stencil card
handmade paper
clear oil- or water-based satin varnish

1 Paint the screen with one coat of parchment-coloured matt emulsion paint, using a medium paintbrush. Leave to dry completely, then apply a second coat of paint.

2 The screen is decorated with squares of tissue paper, so mark vertical and horizontal guidelines over the screen using a pencil, tape measure and ruler.

3 Spray the sheets of tissue paper with gold paint. Stick down squares of tissue on to the screen using a paintbrush and wallpaper paste or PVA glue.

4 Cut pieces of tissue paper to fit the curved top edge of the screen and glue in place. Make colour photocopies of real leaves and flowers. Carefully cut out the shapes using a craft knife and cutting mat.

5 Select some dried flowers and leaves to decorate the curved top panels of the screen.

6 Arrange the leaf and flower photocopies on the screen and glue in position.

7 Arrange the dried flowers and leaves on the curved top sections and glue in place.

8 Make a tooth-edged pattern template out of stencil card. Use this to cut out strips of edging from handmade paper.

9 Glue the strips to the edges of the screen. When the glue is dry, cover the screen with two coats of satin varnish, leaving to dry between coats.

VEG-TABLE

A small table fits in anywhere – in the living room, the kitchen or the conservatory. These chilli peppers make a colourful decoration for a table with an easily achieved distressed paint finish. Experiment with different paint colours and decorate with your favourite vegetables.

YOU WILL NEED
wooden table
emulsion paint: white, green and yellow
large and medium paintbrushes
soft cloth
wax
fine-grade sandpaper
tape measure
colour pictures of vegetables
craft knife
cutting mat
small, sharp scissors
piece of plastic
PVA glue
clear water-based acrylic satin varnish

1 Paint the table with white emulsion paint using a large paintbrush. Leave to dry. Next paint with green emulsion and leave to dry.

2 Using a soft cloth, rub wax unevenly over the surface of the table. Leave to dry.

3 Paint the table with yellow emulsion and leave to dry completely.

4 Using fine-grade sandpaper, gently rub the surface of the table until you can see the green paint showing through. Sand the surface until the desired distressed look is achieved.

5 Measure the surface of the table so that you know how much to enlarge the vegetables. You may find it helpful to make a newspaper pattern so that you can estimate how many photocopies you need.

6 Photocopy the vegetable pictures. Start by cutting out the small inner areas of the vegetable design using a craft knife and cutting mat. Take care not to tear any of the delicate stems.

7 Cut out larger pieces with a small pair of scissors, taking care not to break the delicate stems.

8 Arrange the vegetables and leaves on the table until you are happy with the design.

▶

9 Pick up the cut-outs one at a time and turn upside down on to a piece of plastic to apply the glue. Gently pick each piece up and lay it down on the table, taking care to smooth the surface gently and making sure there are no creases.

10 To finish, varnish with about four coats of clear satin varnish, leaving each coat to dry before applying the next.

TAKE A LETTER

Many of the images used in decoupage can be found in black-and-white source books. These are photocopied and can then be hand-tinted with paints; the leaves on this letter rack have been given a golden, autumnal hue which is enhanced by the gold leaf.

YOU WILL NEED
unpainted letter rack
green emulsion paint
medium and small paintbrushes
small, sharp scissors
craft knife
cutting mat
acrylic paint: red, yellow ochre
and umber
Japanese gold size
Dutch gold leaf transfer book
soft cloths
PVA glue
clear water-based acrylic satin varnish
stained wax

1 Paint the letter rack with green emulsion paint using a medium paintbrush. Leave to dry, then apply a second coat of green emulsion paint.

2 Photocopy the leaves at the back of the book and carefully cut them out. Use small, sharp scissors for the outside edges and a craft knife and cutting mat for the fiddly inside areas.

3 Hand-tint the leaves using diluted acrylic paint in red, yellow ochre and umber and a fine paint-brush. Use thin washes of colour.

4 Paint Japanese gold size on to the top edge of each section of the letter rack. Work over the edge and paint a line roughly the width of your brush. Leave to dry until the size is still slightly tacky. ▶

5 Cut the Dutch gold leaf into strips and gently press on to the Japanese gold size. Allow to dry, then rub off any excess with a dry soft cloth.

6 Arrange the tinted leaves in a pattern on the three sections of the rack and glue in place so that they slightly overlap the gold lines.

7 Varnish with three coats of clear satin varnish, allowing the varnish time to dry thoroughly between each coat.

8 Rub on stained wax, quite thickly to get into the edges of the paper. Allow to dry a little, then rub off the wax to leave a nice sheen.

DECOUPAGE DOOR KNOBS

An old chest of drawers can be transformed with a lick of paint and brightly coloured knobs.
Make the knobs stand out with a different mini decoupage image for each one. Match the images
to the contents of the drawer or just choose pictures that take your fancy.

YOU WILL NEED
wooden knobs
emulsion paint in bright colours
small paintbrushes
PVA glue
imitation gold leaf paper
small, sharp scissors
craft knife
pictures from magazines and wrapping paper
pencil
cutting mat
coloured paper
clear water-based acrylic matt varnish
screwdriver and screws

1 Paint each wooden knob in a different colour of paint using a small brush. Dilute the PVA glue half and half with water.

2 For the blue knob, cut a rough square of imitation gold leaf paper with scissors. Pick it up with a craft knife. Brush the surface of the knob with glue and lightly stick the gold paper to the knob. Press down very gently with your finger. Leave it to dry completely. Cut out a heart and glue it in the centre.

3 For the orange knob, draw a set of five rings, one inside the other, on to the back of a picture. Using a craft knife and cutting mat, cut out the rings. Apply glue to the knob, then stick the centre circle, the middle ring and the outer ring on to the knob with the right side showing.

4 For the yellow knob, cut two narrow strips of paper and apply glue to the back. Arrange them at right angles across the knob. Make sure the strips end under the wide part of the knob. Glue a motif to the centre to cover the join.

5 Decorate the remaining knobs with motifs cut from magazines and wrapping paper. Finish with several coats of varnish, leaving each coat to dry completely before applying the next.

6 Screw the knobs on to your chosen piece of furniture.

Right: The range of options for decorating your door knobs, from swirls and circles to strong graphic images and floral designs, is endless.

TRAY MAGNIFIQUE

The lovable dog looks very grand surrounded by golden ropes and tassels. This fun project combines decoupage with stencilling techniques. Choose a rich background paint colour for the tray to offset the black-and-white photocopy.

YOU WILL NEED
unpainted wooden tray
red emulsion paint
medium and small paintbrushes
scissors
craft knife
cutting mat
PVA glue
sheet of acetate
permanent black pen
stencil brush
acrylic paint: gold and white
clear water-based acrylic satin varnish
antique pine acrylic varnish

1 Paint the wooden tray with red emulsion paint using a medium paintbrush. Apply a second coat if necessary.

2 Photocopy the dog motif at the back of the book, enlarging it as necessary, and cut out with scissors.

3 Cut out the fiddly inner areas using a craft knife and cutting mat.

4 Glue the dog motif in the centre of the tray. Leave to dry.

5 Scale up the cord and tassel templates at the back of the book and draw them on to a sheet of acetate with a permanent black pen.

6 Carefully cut out the stencils with a craft knife and cutting mat.

7 Using a stencil brush and gold acrylic paint, stipple the straight cord stencil all around the edge of the tray to frame the dog, using the corner stencil at each corner.

8 Stencil two tassels in one of the top corners of the tray, and one below the bottom border.

9 Using the same stencils, highlight the cord and tassel with white acrylic paint. Leave to dry.

10 Finish the tray with three coats of clear acrylic varnish, leaving to dry completely between coats. Finally, paint on a coat of antique pine acrylic varnish.

DOOR PLAQUE

It can be difficult to find door plaques, other than plain white, to suit contemporary homes. A clear glass plaque allows you to choose any design you like using motifs cut from greetings cards, wrapping paper or magazines. This quick project is ideal for beginners.

YOU WILL NEED
clear glass plaque
cardboard
craft knife
cutting mat
ruler
block of wood
masking tape
gold spray paint
pencil
magazine pictures and greetings cards
PVA glue
clear water-based acrylic satin varnish
screwdriver and screws

1 Cut a rectangle of cardboard slightly bigger than the plaque, using a craft knife, cutting mat and ruler.

2 Tape the rectangle of cardboard on to the wood.

3 Spray with several thin coats of gold paint. Check the manufacturer's instructions - using with a primer gives a much bolder colour.

4 Draw a pencil line around the shape of the plaque in the centre of the cardboard.

5 If using greetings cards, peel off the thick backing paper with a craft knife to make the paper thinner and easier to work with.

6 Dilute the PVA glue half and half with water. Arrange the pictures into a pattern on the cardboard panel and glue in place.

7 Cut out the cardboard around the pencil line using a craft knife and ruler. Coat with several layers of varnish, leaving to dry between coats.

8 Place the door plaque over the decorated panel and fix them both to the door, using screws and a screwdriver.

FRIEZE FRAME

If you can't find a wallpaper border that you like, then why not make your own? Just measure the walls of the room and copy as many motifs as you need to fit. Paint the border to match the colour of your room for a truly individual look.

YOU WILL NEED
lining paper
ruler
craft knife
yellow emulsion paint
medium paintbrushes
PVA glue
small, sharp scissors
green paper
yellow ochre acrylic paint

1 Measure the lining paper to the required length and depth of your frieze. Cut along the edge using a ruler and craft knife.

2 Mix three parts yellow emulsion paint with one part PVA. Add a little water to allow the mixture to flow more easily. Use this to paint the lining paper.

3 Photocopy the frieze motifs at the back of the book enough times to cover the length of the border. Cut them out with scissors.

4 Cut the green paper into equal short lengths. Tear along the top edge to represent greenery.

5 Arrange and glue down the buildings and torn paper along the length of the frieze.

6 Glue down the swag motifs along the top edge of the frieze.

7 Mix a little yellow ochre acrylic paint into some PVA glue. Then dilute four parts tinted glue with one part water.

8 Brush the tinted, diluted glue over the frieze to seal and protect it.

STYLE FILE

Turn a plain folder into a work of art using paper scraps and angelic cut-outs. The angels are stuck on to layers of coloured paper to provide a bold frame. The coloured acrylic varnish gives the finished piece a wonderful aged look like that of old leather.

YOU WILL NEED
black folder
ruler
pencil
papers: orange, rust and black
large and small, sharp scissors
PVA glue
medium paintbrushes
soft cloth
pictures of angels
tinted water-based acrylic satin varnish
craft knife
ribbon

1 Measure the front of the folder and draw a slightly smaller rectangle on orange paper. Tear the paper to size with a ruler to give it a rough edge and cut off the corners.

2 Measure a rectangle of rust paper, smaller than the orange paper to give an even margin all around. Use a ruler to tear the paper to size.

3 Position the rust paper in the centre of the orange and glue in place, rubbing it with a soft cloth to smooth out any wrinkles.

4 Spread PVA glue on to the back of the orange paper. Position and arrange the paper on the folder so that the cut corners allow the corners of the folder to be seen.

5 Cut four strips of black paper to fit inside the orange border and fold into concertinas. Draw a diamond shape on to the front panel of each strip. Cut out, leaving a short join at each folded edge so the diamonds are joined when you open them up.

6 Position and glue the black diamonds along each edge of the folder.

7 Make colour photocopies of the angel pictures. Cut out two large angels to go in the centre of the folder using small, sharp scissors.

8 Cut out small angels using the small scissors. These will frame the two large angels.

9 Position the angels in the centre and around the edge of the folder, and glue in place.

10 Varnish with three or four coats of tinted satin varnish to achieve a leathery look. Finally, make a slit in each side of the folder, close to the edge with a craft knife. Thread a piece of ribbon through each slit from the outside to the inside. Secure with a dab of glue.

ALL SQUARE

An arrangement of simple squares echoing the straight lines of the stool makes this an easy project to attempt. Make sure the pieces of paper are well stuck down and varnished to ensure the stool lives up to the wear and tear of everyday use.

YOU WILL NEED
wooden stool with square top
fine- and medium-grade sandpaper
tape measure
pencil
selection of handmade papers
ruler
gold and patterned papers
craft knife
cutting mat
wallpaper paste
medium paintbrushes
clear oil-based satin varnish

1 Sand down the stool using medium–grade then fine-grade sandpaper.

2 Measure the top of the stool and mark the centre point with a pencil.

3 Measure four squares of handmade paper to cover the top of the stool. Tear out the paper using a ruler to make the edges slightly uneven.

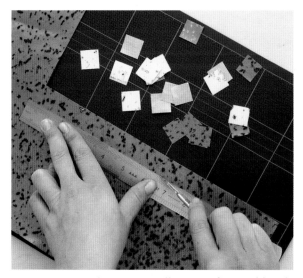

4 Measure and cut out small squares from gold and patterned papers, using a craft knife, ruler and cutting mat.

5 Mix up a little wallpaper paste according to the manufacturer's instructions. Glue the four large squares of paper on to the stool.

6 When the paper is dry, position the smaller squares on top and glue in place.

7 Measure the edges and sides of the stool and cut pieces of handmade and gold paper to fit. Glue them in place.

8 Position small paper squares around the sides of the stool and glue in place.

9 Work around the stool, making sure all the squares are well glued down.

10 When the paste is completely dry, cover with several coats of clear satin varnish.

WASTEPAPER BIN

This wastepaper bin is appropriately decorated with waste paper. Paint the bin in a strong background colour, then cut out and arrange a selection of paper shapes to form a pleasing pattern. You will need to use a drill with a metal bit for this project.

YOU WILL NEED
metal bin
mauve eggshell emulsion paint
medium and small paintbrushes
three wooden knobs (for feet)
drill with metal drill bits
metal file
screwdriver and three screws
natural-coloured paper
ruler
craft knife
cutting mat
masking tape
markor pon
PVA glue
kitchen paper
clear oil-based satin varnish

1 Paint the bin with two coats of mauve eggshell emulsion paint. Leave to dry.

2 Paint the doorknobs to match the bin.

3 Drill three holes in the base of the bin and remove any sharp edges with a metal file. Screw the knobs to the base of the bin.

4 Cut narrow strips of paper, using a ruler, craft knife and cutting mat, and arrange them temporarily with pieces of masking tape. ▶

5 Using a marker pen, draw tall triangles on the paper, then cut them out.

6 Glue the diagonal strips of paper on to the bin. Pat in place with kitchen paper. Trim the ends with a craft knife.

7 Add the paper triangles to the top edge of the bin. Glue a wide strip of paper around the base.

8 Finish with three coats of clear varnish, inside and out, for protection, leaving each coat to dry before applying the next.

TAKE A SEAT

Create a technicolour dream of a chair using an array of colourful papers. Tear papers into even pieces, wrap around the chair and glue in place. This rather time-consuming project will certainly be a talking point when it is finished.

YOU WILL NEED
chair
medium-grade sandpaper
wrapping paper
ruler
PVA glue
small and medium paintbrushes
kitchen paper
small, sharp scissors
clear oil-based satin varnish
fabric to cover seat
staple gun

1 Sand down the chair with medium-grade sandpaper to provide a key for the glue.

2 Tear strips of wrapping paper using a ruler, to give soft edges to the strips.

3 Apply plenty of glue to the back of the paper pieces and start to cover the chair.

4 Continue to glue the paper pieces on to the chair, overlapping them very slightly to avoid gaps but avoiding bulky joins. Smooth down firmly with a pad of kitchen paper to remove any air bubbles.

5 Tear strips of paper to fit neatly over any
awkward areas. Apply glue to the back of the
paper, then when lightly stuck on, apply more glue
over the top of the paper to make it slippery. Slide the
paper into position, being careful not to tear it.

6 Choose a strong motif for the focal point of the
chair and press down, unglued, with your fingers.
Get an imprint of the shape on the chair, then remove
and cut out in detail with scissors. Glue in place.
Leave to dry.

7 Varnish liberally, paying particular attention to the
parts which will get most wear and tear.

8 Cover the chair seat with fabric, securing the
edges with a staple gun.

MIRROR MIRROR

An MDF mirror frame becomes a work of art when decorated with simple strips of wrapping paper. Apply crackle varnish and gold powder to make it extra special. The variety of techniques necessary for this project make it suitable for a more experienced craftworker.

YOU WILL NEED
mirror tile and sticky fixer pads
pencil, ruler and felt-tipped pen
8mm/¼in MDF (medium-density fibreboard)
jigsaw and protective mask
wood glue
wrapping paper
craft knife
cutting mat
PVA glue
small and medium paintbrushes
spray adhesive
craquelure varnish
gold powder
soft cloth
spray fixative
clear oil-based satin varnish
drill with wood drill bits
string
picture rings and chain
screwdriver

1 Draw around the mirror tile on to MDF and add a 9 cm/3½in border all around. Cut a back and a front panel to this size using a jigsaw. Cut out the centre of the front panel. Cut a plaque 8.5 x 18 cm/3¼ x 7 in. (Always wear a mask when cutting MDF because of the fine dust it creates.) Glue the panels together using wood glue.

2 Cut strips of wrapping paper in varying widths using a craft knife, ruler and cutting mat and arrange them on the frame front. Glue in place with PVA glue.

3 To make each corner piece, hold a piece of paper on to the frame and press around the edges. Remove and cut out the corner section. Glue the back of the paper and fold over the edges of the frame.

4 Draw two decorative swirls on the back of the paper with a felt-tipped pen. Cut out using a craft knife and cutting mat.

5 Place the swirls on a piece of scrap paper and spray with adhesive. Glue on to two corners of the frame.

6 Apply the two coats of craquelure varnish, following the manufacturer's instructions, to give a crackle finish to the frame.

7 Rub gold powder into the cracks with a cloth, using small amounts at a time. Rub off any excess. Seal the frame with fixative. Decorate the hanging plaque in the same way as the frame. Coat both the frame and the hanging plaque with varnish. ▶

8 Drill two holes in the bottom of the frame and in the top of the hanging plaque. Join the two together with string, knotting the ends at the front.

9 Stick the mirror in place using sticky pads.

10 Attach the picture rings and chain to the back.

WOODEN BOX

This beautiful box can be used for keeping special photographs, letters and mementoes. Choose faces and lettering from wrapping paper or prints and combine with a collage of handmade paper scraps in toning colours. The finished box is colourwashed to give it an aged look.

YOU WILL NEED
wooden box
fine-grade sandpaper
reproductions of "old master" drawings of faces, animals and lettering
tracing paper
pencil
handmade uncoloured Japanese paper
carbon paper
wallpaper paste or PVA glue
small, medium and large paintbrushes
watercolour paints
magazine pictures
scissors
stencil card
ruler
craft knife
cutting mat
decorator's sponge
burnt umber acrylic paint
clear oil-based matt varnish

1 Sand the box with fine-grade sandpaper to get a smooth surface, and clean the metal hinges and catches of the box.

2 Make photocopies of reproductions of "old master" drawings. Trace over the images and transfer them on to pieces of handmade paper.

3 Alternatively, you can photocopy the image and place carbon paper face down on the handmade paper. Draw over the image so that the trace comes through on to the handmade paper.

4 When you have traced a selection of images, tear them out roughly. Also tear up some plain handmade paper into irregular pieces. Arrange the images on the box.

5 Glue down the pieces, completely covering the surface of the box. Make coloured photocopies of different types of lettering. Glue photocopies of old parchment on to the box, too.

6 Handpaint some motifs of your own, to add touches of colour and interest. Leave to dry, then cut roughly or tear round these images and glue on to the box.

7 Glue on any other details cut or photocopied from colour magazines.

8 Design and cut out a stencil pattern for the edges from stencil card, using a craft knife and cutting mat.

9 Use a sponge to stencil the border pattern on to handmade paper with water-colour paint.

10 Enhance the images on the box with touches of watercolour paints and wash over the entire surface with an antiquing colour such as diluted burnt umber acrylic paint.

11 Finish with a coat of clear matt varnish.

STILL LIFE

Classic Dutch tulips captured in a still life have a timeless appeal. Create your own decoupage flower arrangement and preserve it forever on a small box, a table top or a tray. The design is simple but some care is needed to apply the pieces accurately.

YOU WILL NEED
small cardboard box with lid
emulsion paint: white and yellow
medium and small paintbrushes
reproduction of an old flower print
small, sharp scissors
PVA glue
green paper
ruler
craft knife
cutting mat
clear water-based acrylic satin varnish

1 Paint the box and lid with white emulsion and leave to dry. Next, paint it with two coats of yellow emulsion.

2 Make colour photocopies of the print and carefully cut out the flowers using a pair of small, sharp scissors.

3 Arrange the flowers on the lid. Keep the stems close together to form a bunch. Glue them down using a small brush to apply the glue.

4 Cut out a rectangle of green paper. Fold it in half lengthways and then in half again. Using a small pair of scissors, cut three small triangles from the folded edge. Open out the paper and glue in place on the lid to form a vase.

▶

5 To match up the flowers on the edge of the lid and the sides of the box, hold each flower against the lid and press to make a crease.

6 Cut along the crease with a craft knife and cutting mat, using a ruler as a guide.

7 Glue the flower on to the edge of the lid, then line up the flower on the box side and glue in place. Add more flowers around the box.

8 Varnish the finished box with three or four coats of clear satin varnish, leaving to dry completely between coats.

COAT RACK

This contemporary design, using images taken from books, magazines and posters, is perfect for children's rooms. Woodworking skills are needed to make the rack, although you could simply decorate a ready-made rack. Let each child create their own montage.

YOU WILL NEED
10 mm/³⁄₈ in thick MDF (medium-density fibreboard)
ruler
pencil
jigsaw and a protective mask
duck-egg blue emulsion paint
medium and small paintbrushes
magazine pictures
craft knife
cutting mat
plain coloured paper
PVA glue
three wooden knobs
silver acrylic paint
drill and wood drill bits
screwdriver and three countersunk screws
clear water-based acrylic matt varnish
two mirror plates and screws

1 Following the diagram at the back of the book, draw out the shape of the coat rack on MDF with a ruler and pencil. Cut out using a jigsaw.

2 Paint the coat rack with two coats of duck-egg blue emulsion, leaving the paint to dry completely between coats.

3 Cut out pictures from magazines using a craft knife and cutting mat.

4 Cut three 10 cm/4 in diameter circles of plain paper. Glue the backs and position them along the base of the rack below each point.

5 Arrange the motifs on the rack and, when you are happy with the arrangement, stick them down. Start with your favourite images and arrange the rest to complement these. ▶

6 Paint the knobs with silver acrylic paint and leave to dry.

7 Drill three holes in the rack, one through the centre of each paper circle. Countersink the holes on the back of the rack. Use countersunk screws to attach the knobs to the rack. Varnish the complete rack and leave to dry.

8 Fix a mirror plate to each end of the back of the rack.

PLACE SETTINGS

Decorate new unpainted mats or renovate worn ones with a paint effect and decoupage decoration.
The background creates the impression of raw silk to complement the Chinese print. The rather
time-consuming techniques will provide beautiful results for the more advanced decoupage artist.

YOU WILL NEED
set of place-mats
water-based traditional paint: bright blue and pale green
medium and small paintbrushes
clear water-based acrylic dead-flat varnish
glaze medium
kitchen paper
white French polish
photocopy of a Chinese print
craft knife
cutting mat
small, sharp scissors
pencil
paper glue
permanent ink gold pen
shellac
clear satin varnish
gold wax
clear polyurethane matt varnish

1 Paint the surface of each mat with quick-drying
water-based traditional paint in bright blue using
sideways strokes. Leave to dry, then seal with dead-flat
water-based varnish.

2 Using pale green traditional paint mixed with a
little glaze medium, paint over the whole surface
of the mat using sideways strokes again. With a pad of
kitchen paper wipe away some areas in the direction
of the brushstrokes. The aim is to give the impression
of raw silk. The glaze will slow down the drying and
give you time to experiment. When you are satisfied
with the results, leave to dry. Seal with dead-flat
acrylic varnish.

3 Seal the coloured Chinese print with white French polish using a pad of kitchen paper. Carefully cut out the motifs first with a craft knife and then cut round the outside of the shape with small scissors. In order to avoid tearing, small details, such as the righthand basket, can be cut off and rejoined at the gluing stage.

4 Decide where the print is to go, lightly mark with a pencil and then apply paper glue to this area of the mat. Work the glue over the surface with your finger so that it forms an even film. Position the print and gently rub it with your finger to make sure it is well stuck down. Check that there are no air bubbles or wrinkles. Leave to dry overnight and then remove all surplus glue from the surface.

5 Photocopy the border motifs from the back of the book. Colour in the border motifs with gold pen and seal with shellac. Leave to dry and carefully cut out with a craft knife, cutting the centre areas first. Glue the corner pieces to the mat, 2.5 cm/1 in from the edge. (If you are planning to decorate a whole set of mats, it is a good idea to make a border template from strips of paper 2.5 cm/1 in wide to save constant measuring.)

6 Draw a gold line around the edge of the mat using the curved corner of another mat as a template. Cover with up to 12 coats of clear satin varnish, leaving it to dry between coats.

▶

7 Rub gold wax around the edge of the mat and then apply two coats of clear matt varnish over the whole mat to make it heatproof.

Above: Use the same techniques to create a set of differently decorated mats using your own choice of motifs and borders.

CANDLE SHADES

These delicate-looking shades, made from Japanese handmade paper and photocopies of real leaves and flowers, match the soft glow of candlelight. They are treated with fire-proofing spray, but for extra safety, do not leave them unattended when lit.

YOU WILL NEED
Japanese handmade paper
clear oil-based dead-flat varnish
medium and small paintbrushes
pair of compasses
ruler
pencil
card
scissors
selection of fresh and dried flowers
and leaves
craft knife
cutting mat
masking tape
wallpaper paste or PVA glue
decorative paper
fire-proofing spray
candle
candlestick

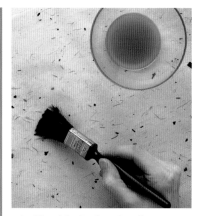

1 Varnish the handmade paper with clear dead-flat varnish and leave to dry.

2 Using a pair of compasses, a ruler and a pencil, draw the shape of the shade on to card, following the design shown in the photograph. Cut out to use as a template. It is a good idea to make a trial shade out of newspaper.

3 Draw around the card template on to the handmade paper and cut out.

4 Make colour photocopies of the flowers and leaves. Carefully cut them out using a craft knife and cutting mat.

5 To plan your design, arrange the cut-outs on the handmade paper, securing them temporarily with masking tape. Glue them in place.

6 Cut out edging details from strips of decorative paper and glue them in place. Leave space at the joining edge. Once the shade is made up, you can add extra pieces to cover the join.

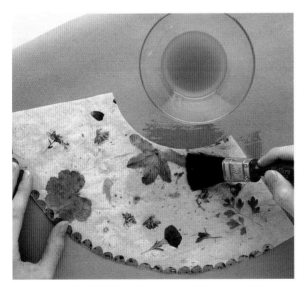

7 Cover the shade with a coat of clear varnish. Leave to dry, then glue the shade together.

8 Draw around the circumference on a piece of card to make the shade support.

9 In the centre of the support, draw a smaller circle for the candle to fit through. Draw intersecting lines through this circle. Then mark four more holes to allow air to circulate. Cut out the support and the small circles.

10 Spray the shade and card with fire-proofing spray.

11 Push the candle through the cardboard support on to the candlestick. Place the shade over the candle to rest on the support.

WALL OF COLOUR

The colourful chequerboard wall is simply painted with sponge scourers before embellishing with cut-out plates and vases. Cheaper than buying all that china – and totally unbreakable, too. This is not a difficult design and can be attempted by a beginner.

YOU WILL NEED
PVA glue
lining paper (or work directly on the wall)
medium and small paintbrushes
white emulsion paint
blue acrylic paint
two sponge scourers
pictures of plates and vases
small, sharp scissors

1 Dilute four parts PVA glue with one part water. Brush on to the lining paper or wall to seal the surface.

2 Paint with white emulsion and leave to dry.

3 On a plate, mix a little blue acrylic paint into the white emulsion to make a pale blue.

4 Using two sponges, one as a spacer and the other for applying the paint, print a chequerboard pattern over the wall or paper. Practise the technique on a piece of spare paper first.

5 Make colour photocopies of pictures of plates and vases in different sizes and carefully cut them out with small, sharp scissors.

6 Arrange the photocopies on the chequered background.

7 Glue them in position with the diluted PVA glue. Carefully smooth down the motifs, working from the centre to the edges.

8 Seal the finished design with the diluted PVA to protect the wall.

SHELF LIFE

Bring interest to a forgotten corner with a boldly coloured shelf unit that is easy to decorate. The painted cream- and brown-striped shelves go beautifully with the vase and urn motifs, which are reproductions from a painting by Goya, and are perfect for displaying your own artefacts.

YOU WILL NEED
wooden shelf unit
emulsion paint: white, cream and
chocolate
medium and small paintbrushes
fine-grade sandpaper
pencil
ruler
pictures of jugs and vases
large and small, sharp scissors
PVA glue
clear water-based acrylic satin varnish

1 Paint the shelf unit with two coats of white emulsion, sanding it between the coats.

2 When dry, paint with two coats of cream emulsion.

3 Make faint pencil lines before painting in the chocolate stripes using an artist's brush. Steady your hand by resting it on the edge of the shelf.

4 Paint the edges of the shelf unit with the same chocolate-brown paint.

5 Measure the shelves to gauge the correct height of the photocopies. Make colour photocopies of jugs and vases.

6 Cut out the jugs and vases using large scissors for the outer edges and small scissors for the inside details.

7 Arrange the jugs and vases on the shelf unit, overlapping them a little but without overcrowding the images.

8 Glue down the first layer of jugs and vases, then glue down the second layer.

9 Finish the shelf with three or four coats of clear acrylic satin varnish.

KEY MATTERS

You'll never lose another key with this sophisticated cupboard to store them in. The cupboard is given a subtle distressed look before finishing with a decorative print. The monkey holding the key is achieved by cutting and cleverly repositioning the image.

YOU WILL NEED
unpainted wooden key cupboard
medium-grade sandpaper
shellac knotting
medium and small paintbrushes
shellac or sanding sealer
water-based traditional paint: deep red and deep blue
clear water-based acrylic dead-flat varnish
candle
fine wire wool
ruler
photocopies of script
craft knife
cutting mat
paper glue
watercolour paints
small, sharp scissors
clear water-based acrylic satin varnish
wax polish and kitchen paper

1 Sand down any rough wood on the cupboard and apply shellac knotting over any knots. Seal the surface with shellac or sanding sealer. Paint the cupboard inside and out with deep red traditional paint and leave to dry. Then seal the surface with a coat of dead-flat varnish.

2 Rub candle wax over the areas where there would be natural wear and tear, such as under the key hole and around the edges of the door, to create a resist.

3 Brush over the outside of the box only in deep blue paint using loose brush strokes. When the paint is completely dry, rub over with fine wire wool. The blue paint will come away over the waxed areas, revealing the red paint underneath.

4 Measure the centre panel on the door and cut a piece of script to this size. Glue in place, checking that there are no air bubbles and that the edges are firmly glued down. Leave to dry overnight. Seal the panel with a coat of dead-flat varnish.

5 Photocopy the key and monkey motifs at the back of the book. Using watercolour paints, tint the monkey with raw umber, deepening some areas to create shadowing. Tint the keys with yellow ochre. Seal all the prints on both sides with white shellac.

6 Choose which key prints you are going to to use inside the box. Cut out, starting with the delicate areas using a craft knife, then use scissors for the outer edges. Arrange the keys inside the box, positioning them about 2 cm/¾ in below where the hooks for the real keys will go. Glue in place by applying the glue to the surface of the box and gently spreading the glue with your finger. Place each key on top and smooth it down, checking that all parts are well stuck down.

7 Cut out the monkey print. If he is to appear to hold the key, cut off the left hand and set it aside. Choose a suitable key and cut it in half. Glue the monkey to the panel and smooth out with your finger. Glue the key to the panel, positioning it either side of the hand to make it look realistic. Leave to dry.

8 Clean off any surplus glue. Paint over the prints with up to 12 coats of clear satin varnish, allowing two hours drying time between coats. Wax with a good-quality wax polish.

Above: Decoupage is a delightful way of assembling images. Here, the bird and butterfly are made to sit on the branch.

MATERIALS

The materials needed for decoupage are inexpensive and readily available from arts and crafts stores. The basic items are listed here; more specialized requirements are given in the lists of materials for individual projects.

CUTTINGS

Images for decoupage can be gleaned from a many sources such as wrapping paper, prints, newspapers, greetings cards and catalogues. They can be photo-copied in black and white and colourwashed in your own choice of colours, or colour copied to make endless duplicates for a frieze or set of mats. Start a collection of decoupage images, motifs and pictures that catch your eye so you will always have a store of cuttings from which to choose.

GLUES

Paper glue is a golden-coloured liquid glue that comes in a bottle. It is ideal for paper projects, although it may be slower to dry than other glues.

PVA glue is a white glue that dries quickly to a clear finish. It can be used full strength or diluted as required (see individual project instructions). It can also be diluted to use as a sealer on finished decoupage projects.

Wood glue may be required for some of the projects involving woodwork. It is a stronger form of PVA glue.

Spray adhesive gives a light, even application of glue. Always work in a well-ventilated area when using this type of glue.

Wallpaper paste is easy to mix up and use for larger projects, but it is not as strong as PVA glue. It contains fungicide, which prevents mould. It has a slippery feel, ideal for moving the decoupage motifs into an accurate position.

PAINTS

Acrylic paints come in a range of colours. Ideal for applying colour highlights, acrylic paints can be used full strength or diluted with water or an acrylic medium. Mixing with an acrylic medium gives a stronger colour.

Emulsion paints are used for most of the projects in this book. They come in a wide variety of colours and dry quickly.

Traditional paints come in a range of subtle colours and dry to a chalky finish similar to the old-fashioned casein or milk paints. They need sealing with a coat of acrylic varnish before the next coat is applied.

VARNISHES

These are available as oil-based polyurethane varnishes or water-based acrylic varnishes. Both types are available in gloss, satin (mid-sheen) or matt finishes. Acrylic varnish has the advantage of not yellowing with age.

Shellac dries to a transparent finish. It is less hardwearing than varnish and tends to be used between layers rather than as a finishing sealer.

OTHER MATERIALS

Masking tape is used for screening off areas before painting and also for temporarily fixing the motifs while arranging them.

Wood filler is necessary for filling any holes in furniture or other wooden items before applying the decoupage motifs. Sand down the dried filler to ensure a smooth surface.

White spirit is a clear solvent used for diluting oil-based paints, washing brushes and cleaning objects to be decoupaged.

Spiralling from top left: traditional paints, acrylic paints, acrylic varnish, wallpaper paste, masking tape, shellac, cuttings, paper glue, wood glue, wood filler, white spirit, oil-based varnish, emulsion paint and PVA glue.

EQUIPMENT

Apart from a pair of small, sharp scissors and a selection of paintbrushes in different sizes, there are very few pieces of equipment that are needed for decoupage projects. Where woodwork techniques are needed to make the base of a project, the extra equipment is listed.

PAINTBRUSHES

The key to good paintwork is choosing the correct paintbrush. The three main types of brushes are household or decorator's, artist's and stencil brushes, and each type comes in a wide variety of shapes and sizes.

Household brushes should be used for painting basecoats and applying varnishes, and artist's brushes for fine paintwork. You can buy specialist varnishing brushes, although household ones are perfectly adequate.

Artist's brushes are used for hand-tinting prints and adding intricate decoration.

Stencil brushes are used when a decoupage project also uses stencilled images.

Always ensure a different brush is used for the varnish and the paintwork, otherwise the varnish will have flecks of paint in it.

Buy the best-quality paintbrush you can or the work may be spoilt by loose hairs caught in the varnish.

Clean brushes immediately after use; clean them in water if the paint or varnish is water-based or in white spirit if the paint or varnish is oil-based.

CUTTING EQUIPMENT

For decoupage, you will need a pair of small, sharp scissors to cut around intricate motifs and a pair of larger scissors for cutting out templates and larger pieces of paper and card.

Some people prefer to use a scalpel or craft knife as these are particularly good for cutting out intricate patterns. The blades are extremely sharp; they should always be used with a cutting mat so that the knife does not slip or damage your work surface. Replace the blade regularly so that it remains sharp and gives you a good, clean outline.

OTHER EQUIPMENT

Sandpaper comes in various grades from fine to coarse. Use a fine-grade paper for rubbing down between coats of paint and use a coarser paper for preparing surfaces before you begin your decoupage.

Tweezers are useful for picking up very delicate cut-outs, which may get damaged in your fingers.

Metal rulers are essential if you are cutting along a straight edge with a scalpel because the blade will make nicks in a plastic ruler and then the line will not be straight. Metal rulers are also useful for cutting paper when you want a softer edge than can be made by scissors. A metal or plastic ruler can be used for measuring and designing projects.

A pair of compasses is sometimes needed for designing projects.

A pencil or felt-tipped pen and paper are needed for planning designs and marking the positions of cut-outs.

Soft cloths, kitchen paper and dish cloths are useful for rubbing down images and removing excess glue from the surface.

Access to a black-and-white and a colour photocopier is also very useful because you may need to make large numbers of copies.

Clockwise from top left: cutting mat, tweezers, scalpel, craft knife, pair of compasses, metal ruler, tape measure, plastic ruler, felt-tipped pen, pencil, stencil brush, artist's paintbrushes, household paintbrushes, soft cloth, dish cloth, kitchen paper, medium-grade and fine-grade sandpaper, large scissors and small, sharp scissors.

TECHNIQUES

*The techniques of decoupage are very simple and are quickly learned. The most important skill is
that of carefully cutting out and handling the paper cutting. The project shown here covers all the
basic processes involved in decoupage.*

PREPARING SURFACES

1 For older and worn wooden items, it is essential to wipe the surface with white spirit, then fill any nicks with wood filler, following the manufacturer's instructions.

2 Sand down the object with sandpaper until smooth and seal with shellac.

3 Wipe away any dust with white spirit so that you have a clean surface.

4 Prime the object with two coats of white emulsion paint. An additional colour can then be painted on top.

SEALING

5 Seal the image with a coat of shellac painted on to the paper. The images may be wrapping paper, colour or black-and-white photocopies or one-off pictures. Shellac also stiffens delicate images, making them easier to cut out and preventing discoloration.

CUTTING

6 Cut roughly around the image with a pair of large scissors.

7 Then cut around the edge of the image with a smaller pair of scissors. For delicate images, hold the paper in your hand and rotate it as you cut the curves. Always use a ruler to tear straight edges.

8 To cut out internal unwanted paper, use a craft knife and cutting mat. Always take care when using a craft knife.

STICKING

9 Hold and arrange your cut-out images on the painted surface with blobs of low-tack reusable adhesive. This allows you to try different arrangements without damaging and wasting your images.

10 When you are happy with the positioning, glue the motifs on to the background using PVA diluted with a little water.

11 Use a pair of tweezers to pick up delicate images. Place in position, press down and rub over with your fingers or a soft cloth to get rid of any air bubbles or excess glue. Wipe off any excess glue with a damp cloth. Allow to dry.

VARNISHING

12 Varnishing is the final protection. Acrylic varnish is faster-drying and less toxic than oil-based varnish. Seal your finished design with up to twelve coats of clear varnish, giving it a light sanding between coats. The object must be left to dry in a dust-free atmosphere so that it does not pick up any dust particles.

13 Finally, to age an object and to blend the colours, paint on a stained varnish such as antique pine or oak. To get rid of any brushstrokes, rub off the excess stain with a clean cloth, lightly dabbed all over. You can then use a wax polish to give a deep satin feel to the finished piece.

TEMPLATES

Where black and white images or images to be colourwashed are used in the projects, they are provided here. You will need to source colour images yourself. Always measure the object to be decorated and calculate the enlargement necessary before photocopying.

Tray Magnifique, pp 28–31

Hat Trick, pp 8–10

Key Matters, pp 80–83

Take a Letter, pp 22–24

Tray Magnifique, pp 28–31

Place Settings,
pp 66–69

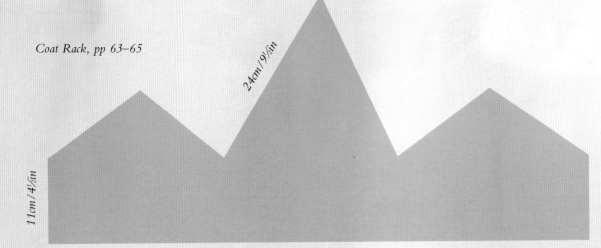

Coat Rack, pp 63–65

24cm/9½in

11cm/4½in

74cm/29in

Frieze Frame, pp 35–37

Key Matters, pp 80–83

SUPPLIERS

Decoupage requires very few specialist materials. The glues, varnishes and paints are available from any good arts supply shop.

The sources of decorative images for decoupage are endless: glossy magazines, postcards, gift cards, books and newspapers, but listed below are a few specialist suppliers. Museums are a wonderful source of books and postcards with reproductions of famous paintings and prints. Interior decorating shops also sell a good range of print material.

The Dover Bookshop
18 Earlham Street
London WC2H 9LN
UK
Tel: 0171 836 2111
Sells a wide range of source books

Ornamenta
3–12 Chelsea Harbour Design Centre, Chelsea Harbour
London SW10 OXE
UK
Tel: 0171 352 1824
Border designs, cherubs and print room decorations

Panduro Hobby Ltd
West Way House
Transport Avenue
Brentford
Middx TW8 9HF
UK
Tel: 0181 847 6161
Hat boxes by mail order

Hawkin & Co.
Saint Margaret
Harleston
Norfolk IP20 OPJ
UK
Tel: 01986 782536
Suppliers of decoupage scraps by mail order

Dover Publications Inc.
31 East 2nd Street
Mineola, NY 11501
USA
Tel: 516 294 7000
Publishers of Dover Books

General Publishing
30 Lesmill Road
Donmills
Toronto
Canada
Tel: 416 445 3333
Distributors of Dover Books

Rosenhain, Lipmann & Peers
147 Burnley Street
Richmond
Melbourne
Victoria 3121
Australia
Paper products and scraps

ACKNOWLEDGEMENTS

The publishers would like to thank the following people for designing the projects in this book: Catherine Macdonald for the Hat Trick, pp 8–10, Veg-Table pp 18–21, Frieze Frame pp 35–37, Style File pp 38–41, Still Life pp 60–62, Wall of Colour pp 74–76, Shelf Life pp 77–79; Josephine Whitfield for the Shell Collection pp 11–13, Take a Letter pp 22–24, Tray Magnifique pp 28–31 and the Techniques; Kerry Skinner of Rare Creation for the Screen Test pp 14–17, All Square pp 42–45, Wooden Box pp 56–59 and Candle Shades pp 70–73; Sandra Hadfield for the Decoupage Door Knobs pp 25–27, Door Plaque pp 32–34, Wastepaper Bin pp 46–48, Take a Seat pp 49–51, Mirror Mirror pp 52–55 and Coat Rack pp 63–65; Elaine Green for Place Settings pp 66–69 and Key Matters pp 80–83.

INDEX